EAST

COMMONWEALTH AVENUE

WALNUT STREET

SOUTH OFFICE BUILDING

CAPITOL EAST WING

CAPITOL ANNEX

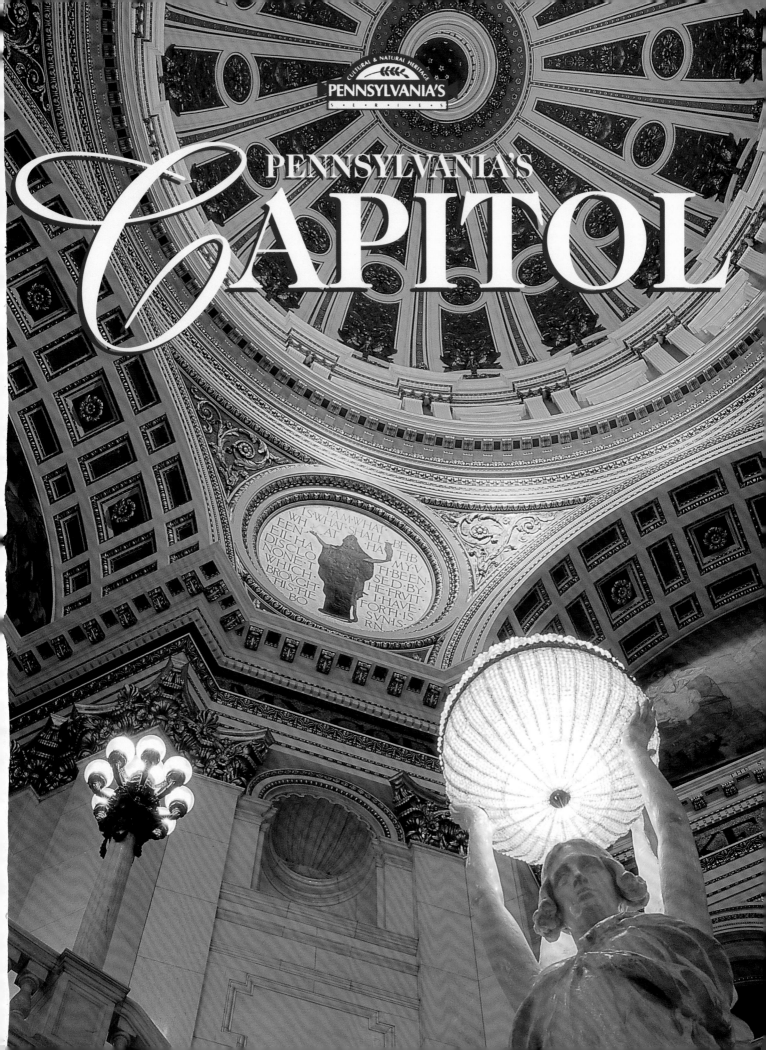

CULTURAL & NATURAL HERITAGE
PENNSYLVANIA'S
S · E · R · I · E · S

PENNSYLVANIA'S
CAPITOL

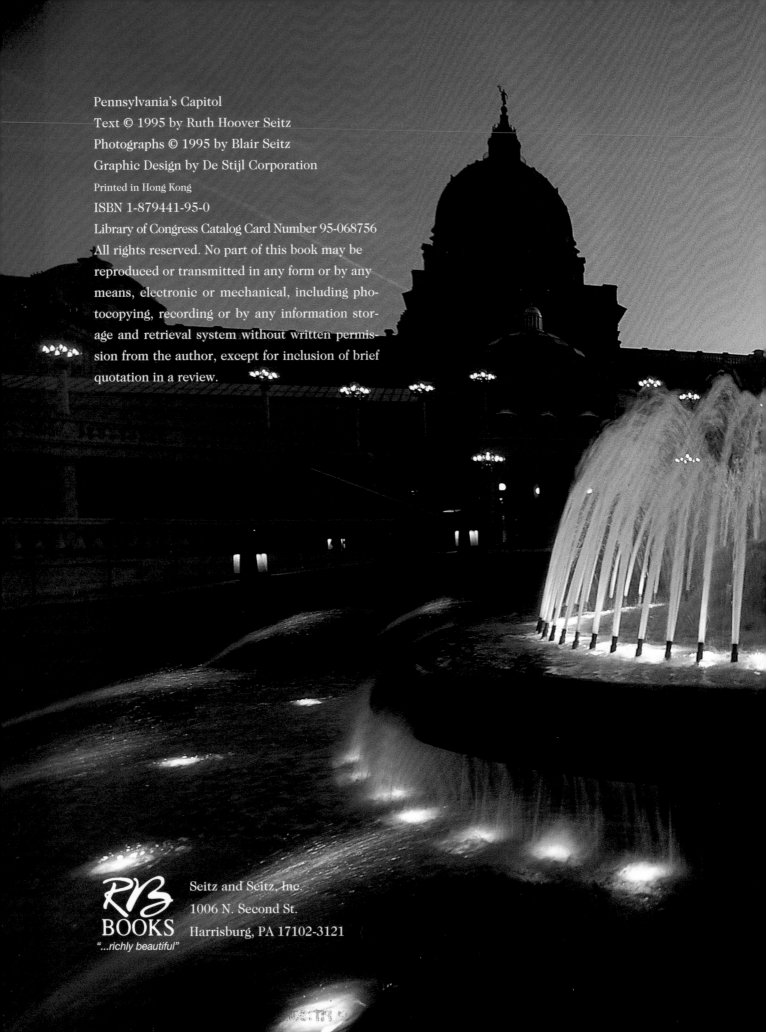

Pennsylvania's Capitol

Text © 1995 by Ruth Hoover Seitz

Photographs © 1995 by Blair Seitz

Graphic Design by De Stijl Corporation

Printed in Hong Kong

ISBN 1-879441-95-0

Library of Congress Catalog Card Number 95-068756

RB BOOKS
"...richly beautiful"

Seitz and Seitz, Inc.
1006 N. Second St.
Harrisburg, PA 17102-3121

PENNSYLVANIA'S
CAPITOL

RB
BOOKS
"...richly beautiful"

HARRISBURG, PA

SOUTH SIDE BRANCH

FOREWORD

uilt in the first decade of the twentieth century, our state-house stands as a monument to the new Renaissance in America. Architect Joseph M. Huston borrowed from a plethora of European traditions, blending classical and Renaissance forms and motifs with Pennsylvania themes to produce something uniquely American. His vision for the Pennsylvania Capitol extended beyond the architectural design of the building. Huston believed, as did many of his contemporaries, that the ideals of the Renaissance were expressed in the unified effort of painters, sculptors and craftsmen, all orchestrated by the guiding vision and spirit of the architect.

In 1982 the Capitol Preservation Committee was established by the Pennsylvania General Assembly to coordinate and oversee programs to conserve, restore, preserve and maintain the State Capitol and its historic contents. As a result of one legislator's active interest in the history of the Capitol, the concept of the Committee actually preceded its creation by several years. While walking into the Capitol from a parking lot, Representative Matthew J. Ryan noticed a discarded, original marble fireplace near a dumpster for garbage pickup. When Ryan became Speaker of the House in 1981, he and Democratic Leader K. Leroy Irvis rallied support for the establishment of a bipartisan committee to restore and preserve the Capitol in time for the 75th anniversary of the building's dedication.

Since its inception, the Capitol Preservation Committee has completed over 50 projects under the dedicated leadership of Chairman Joseph R. Pitts. The Committee's efforts have won historic preservation awards and made international art news for the innovative conservation of the Rotunda Dome and Murals.

The Pennsylvania Capitol is not a pristine museum, but the functioning center of the Commonwealth's government. Maintaining the building's historical integrity, the Capitol Preservation Committee moves forward with reverence. With every chandelier that is relamped and every mural that is cleaned and restored, a piece of Pennsylvania's past glory is preserved for future generations.

Ruthann Hubbert-Kemper
Ruthann Hubbert-Kemper
Director, Capitol Preservation Committee

$\mathscr{C}$ONTENTS

▣ ***Following Pages:*** *With the Susquehanna River flowing to the west, an aerial view features the integrated design of the Capitol Complex with the East Wing (1987) in the shadow of the Main Capitol (1906) and flanked by the South (1921) and North (1929) Office Buildings.*

GOVERNMENT ON A HILL

Pennsylvanians rightly prize their domed Capitol building which is situated prominently on a rise in the heart of Harrisburg. When people climb the 45 steps from Third Street to the bronze doors of the main entrance on the west facade, they sense the grandeur of its American Beaux Arts style which echoes the ornate classicism of past centuries. The colossal granite structure embraces the varied European influences that united in the architecture of the American Renaissance.

Its overall elegance was underlined at the dedication in 1906 when President Theodore Roosevelt called the Capitol "the handsomest building I ever saw." Today, visitors still voice appreciation for its splendid architecture and rich decorative art. Travelers who have visited all 50 of America's statehouses commonly say that Pennsylvania's is the most beautiful.

During its early years, Pennsylvania's government moved frequently. Originally, William Penn had planned to make Upland (now Chester) his colony's capital, but upon arrival in 1682 the founder

decided to move it farther up the Delaware. He called it Philadelphia. For years, the colony's Assembly and Council met in various homes, Quaker meetinghouses and a school. Six years after deciding to build its own State House in 1729, the legislature first convened in what was the largest and most imposing building in the Colonies, Independence Hall.

This edifice was more than adequate, but its Philadelphia location was eventually too far from the citizens pushing westward. For at least 20 years legislators discussed possible sites and even relocated to Lancaster in 1799. Finally, an 1810 law designated Harrisburg as the permanent seat of Pennsylvania's government. Selling the old Statehouse to the city of Philadelphia raised $70,000 towards a new Capitol.

The Harrisburg statehouse was to be built on a site that included a four-acre grant set aside much earlier by the town's founder, John Harris. Ten adjoining acres offered by United States Congressman William Maclay and several residential plots completed the property. Its picturesque location was high enough that the Capitol could be viewed from the Susquehanna River.

The first Capitol, a brick building, was dedicated January 2, 1822. A parade consisting of architect Stephen Hill (1785-1844), 80 of his workmen, the governor, legislators and other citizens marched two by two to the new Capitol from State Government's intermediate home at the Dauphin County Court House on Market Street.

Sixteen inaugurations later, on February 2, 1897, a raging midday fire destroyed the brick capitol. In April both the House and the Senate passed bills to authorize construction of a new building "... of brick, stone and iron, fire-proof in character." Costs were not to exceed $550,000.

While the work of state government continued in the Grace Methodist Episcopal Church on State Street, a Commission chose the plan of a reputable Chicago architect, Henry Ives Cobb (1859-1931), from among five finalists. But as the building rose, its economical look stirred disappointment, even scorn. It was dubbed a "sugar factory" with one Commission member calling it less attractive than scores of farmers' barns in Pennsylvania.

After much debate, in July of 1901 the Assembly authorized a new design competition to "finish" Cobb's walls. This one was limited to Pennsylvania architects. The completion date was set for 1906, and the budget was increased to $4 million.

The new Capitol Building Commission chose Joseph M. Huston, a 36-year-old relatively inexperienced architect who envisioned creating a "Palace of Art." His aesthetic statement would build on his basic design—a domed central pavilion flanked by longitudinal wings and terminated with transverse wings topped by shallow domes. The memorable edifice would rise on the popular public grounds of Capitol Park, several acres of exotic and native trees, walkways and circular flower beds.

Huston found inspiration for his challenging commission in the great structures of Europe. On an around-the-world trip, his stop in Rome was extended while his brother recovered from an illness. During repeated visits to St Peter's Basilica, the ambitious architect was so overwhelmed by the grandeur of the dome that he "duplicated that inspiration in concrete form." His Capitol dome strikingly resembles the dome of St. Peter's even though its roof is green terra cotta rather than stone and the finial is not a religious cross but Commonwealth, a female figure sculpted by Roland Hinton Perry (1870-1941).

At night the dome sparkles with an airy glitter that belies its 52 million pounds of materials. Streams of light outline the ribs of the domes, the pediments and major cornices. The massive structure is bedded on cement overlaid with seven million bricks, all upheld by four pillars sunk into a natural bed of slate rock.

Simple lines dominate the five-story exterior of gray Vermont granite. Many of the pieces of stone are more than eight feet high and individually weigh up to 35 tons. Granite pieces totaling more than 400,000 cubic feet arrived in Harrisburg via something over 1,100 rail carlaods.

The exterior stretches 525 feet with the structure's tone somber, almost unwelcoming. The relatively austere facade contrasts with the lofty, richly decorated interior where the materials and use of space complement each other with Renaissance richness.

Huston longed to interweave his philosophy of civilization with the history of Pennsylvania to create a

"literature in stone" that would inspire visitors for generations. His design encompassed a wide range of fine arts. Although budget limitations forced him to scale back many of the exterior sculptures, he was still able to achieve a visionary integration of space, color, line and tone in the architectural design as well as in his use of the fine and decorative arts. Not one single element, but the total effect of each area arouses awe. Huston planned for his building of "art in stone" to speak to people of all walks of life.

Choosing to ignore a prevailing notion that discounted local talent, he intentionally sought out Pennsylvania artists. Huston conveyed to them his strong belief in their abilities as well as his focus on Pennsylvania themes with a universal message.

During the initial meeting between Huston and sculptor George Grey Barnard (1863-1938), Barnard grasped the architect's vision within 10 or 12 minutes. Huston wanted the exterior sculptures of the Capitol to be an integral part of this monument to the people.

Ornamentation that honors Pennsylvania's early leaders first greets visitors as they pause at the west entrance to observe the heavy bronze doors. The relief of the design is so intricate because each leaf was cast in a single piece using the "lost wax" process. After making a wax model of the design, the Henry Bonnard Bronze Company of New York coated it with a ceramic material to form a mold and then melted the wax away so that molten metal could be poured into the ceramic mold.

Barnard may have sketched a general scheme for the door design, but Huston's name is engraved on the doors, which were inspired by Ghiberti's doors for the Baptistery in Florence, Italy. A portrait of founder William Penn fills a circle at the top of the arch with scenes below showing his treaty with the Indians and his arrival in the New World. Six panels on the doors illustrate signings of the Declaration of Independence and the Constitution, the domains of History and Education and scenes of mining and agriculture. Ten portrait heads of people involved in building the Capitol frame each door leaf. (When the press protested such egotism, Huston explained that they stood for "types of men," not portraits. Nevertheless, it is obvious that the head that can be lifted to insert the key strongly resembles Huston himself.)

Although each door leaf weighs a ton, the doors were hung with such fine balance that they can be closed with the push of a finger. And since it has always been the intent of the government of Penn's colony and the Keystone State to be "of the people, by the people and for the people," the doors remain ajar as a welcoming gesture. The public can enter freely and enjoy this treasure chest of art which many describe as the number one state capitol in terms of grandeur and architecture.

In front of the main door, Barnard's grouping of human figures oversees the daily flow of human beings. Seven feet high, these white marble statues symbolize the virtues and vices, the yin and yang of human experience. Although a classicist, Barnard considered his sculptures more nearly human than the beautiful forms of the Greeks.

The grouping on the south, "Love and Labor: The Unbroken Law." illustrates positive relationships and activities. The statues are engaged in meaningful work. Interacting people portray happy siblings, supportive young parents and a father forgiving his remorseful son. In contrast, the figures to the north of the entrance allegorically show the loss, brokenness and pain that result from vice and grief.

Barnard claimed that the theme of these statues–the two sides of life, night and day, laws broken and laws kept–meshed while he was walking in the night during a storm, enjoying thunder and lightning.

The significance of the Capitol statues stunned the European art world as soon as they were exhibited in 1910. Barnard was compared to Phidias, Michelangelo and Valasquez. Art critics wrote about "the grandeur of inspiration in the ensemble" and called the sculptor "a master of light and shade."

Barnard's love of sculpture had been awakened in Pennsylvania, his birthplace. As a young teen he travelled by train from the Midwest with his mother in 1876 to the Centennial Exhibition in Philadelphia; there in Memorial Hall his eyes were riveted on an exhibit of sculpture.

As an adult, Barnard remembered sensing "the great hand of God at my back" while he explored the outdoors in his youth, molding the forms of birds in plaster and river clay and then mounting them. To taxidermy he added the skill of engraving. During formal study at the Art Institute of Chicago, he studied busts by Michelangelo, whose style he admired throughout his life.

Intense study in Paris refined Barnard's artistic skills. Despite grueling economic privation there, the young sculptor matured. He was ready for the Capitol commission. The 1902 proposed contract of $700,000 was to have been the largest ever awarded to an American sculptor, but from the beginning difficulties beset the project. The number of figures was whittled down although their size was increased. The final agreement of $100,000 limited Barnard, who worked by sketching and modeling the figures in three sizes of clay before pointing them up in marble to 9 1/2' statuary. The work was only partially completed in 1906 when an investigation

of the financial records of the construction halted the flow of funds.

Another problem was the protest against the nudity of the statues which prompted Barnard to design plaster sheaths as twentieth century fig leaves for the males. He hoped that visitors would "carry away the message of Human Brotherhood as opposed to Human Strife and Greed. Should we allow 'draped' or 'undraped' to minimize that?" He ventured that it might take a hundred years or longer until people could look on God's masterpiece without a blush.

However, all controversy was laid aside for the dedication of the sculptures on October 4, 1911, Barnard Day. Harrisburg schools, factories and government offices closed. Over 800 invited guests and hundreds more gathered along the west facade while drums rolled and a choir of 400 children sang two songs composed for the event. Besides Barnard himself, artists Violet Oakley and William Van Ingen were present. But Huston was not.

The architect who had planned this treasure chest of art was serving a sentence in the Eastern State Penitentiary. As early as 1906, State Treasurer William H. Berry began to uncover gross overbillings for furnishings. A system of invoicing state purchases on a price-per-foot or per-pound basis resulted in a graft scandal that led to Huston's conviction. As architect with an additional contract to furnish the Capitol, Huston had rubberstamped expenditures that skyrocketed the price of the building from $4 million to $13 million. A chief culprit was John H. Sanderson (1854-1909), a Philadelphia furniture seller who received payments of nearly $5.4 million for his "Special Furnishings" contract of $500,000-$800,000. Typical of his overcharges was the $1,619.20 bill for a $75 bootblack stand and two $25 chairs. He had charged the State Treasury for 88 "feet" at a rate of $18.40 per foot. In 1908 Sanderson and four others were indicted on one count of conspiracy to defraud the Commonwealth, but before he was imprisoned, he died alone of illness.

Although Huston claimed innocence, he paid heavily for failing to monitor expenditures more strictly and for his close association with a political machine that misused public funds. After his six-months' prison sentence, Huston never again received a major public commission.

However, after much publicity about misappropriations, substitutions and omissions, in subsequent decades the value of the Capitol and its art gradually rekindled appreciation for Huston's "architectural skill and artistic judgment." Pennsylvanians began to focus on its magnificence rather than its extravagance. One journalist, in an attempt to put the cost of the Capitol in perspective, reminded critics that New York's 1898 capitol had totaled $25 million.

The Capitol, as sumptuous as it was, inevitably began to deteriorate after years of continuous use. Barnard first observed the cracks and discoloration of his figures, which he had carved out of the most durable Blanc Clair marble from Italy. Barnard agonized, "Nothing but the chill of freezing waters and the swelling of ice can account for what has happened." In addition to this weathering, acid rain, sandblasting and dirt accumulation had soiled the Barnard statu-

ary and other sculptures such as the Mexican War Monument, which had been erected in 1868 several decades before the Capitol was built.

The passing of time also adversely affected the interior art. Roof deterioration resulted in moisture and light damage to the Rotunda murals. These and many more restoration projects became the priority of the Capitol Preservation Committee established in 1982.

In that same decade the growth of government required more space. The completion of the East Wing in 1986 added 950,000 square feet of office area and 2½ levels underground parking the size of three

football fields. Its "post-modernist" style by Celli-Flynn Associates/H.F. Lenz Co. blends with the European Renaissance design of the Capitol. Resembling the esplanade of the Vatican, the East Plaza offers places to rest and socialize against a backdrop of multiple glass reflections. The whole project required 76,000 pieces of granite quarried from the same Vermont source used for the Capitol.

The War Veterans Memorial Fountain in the center circulates 35,000 gallons of water. Its computer regulates the design of the water spraying from the nozzles in a pattern that repeats every 20 minutes.

At the completion of the cycle, the water sprays in the shape of a dome.

Directly east of the fountain lies Soldiers' Grove, where mature native red oaks shade the four-acre park. In 1994 a monument of concrete aggregate arcs was dedicated in the Grove to honor the 373 Congressional Medal of Honor recipients from Pennsylvania. The name of each honoree, heroes from the Civil War to the United Nations operations in Somalia, is carved in the granite memorial. Winifred Lutz and Stacy Levy, Pennsylvanians from Huntingdon Valley and Spring Mills, designed this Medal of Honor Memorial, a commemoration unique in the nation.

Citizens often gather on the steps, walkways and grounds of the Capitol. Some come with placards, vehemently demanding that legislators give attention to their cause. Some hold vigils. Others share lunch with friends, even offering scraps to the squirrels in residence. Fourth grade students line up for tours of the statehouse. Families and other groups truly do make the Capitol their own "Palace of Art" seven days of the week. ▨

◉ **Left:** *Situated on a rise in Harrisburg, a midstate city of 53,000, Pennsylvania's Capitol is reflected in the Susquehanna River at dawn.* ◉ **Top:** *Tulips in Soldiers' Grove, a park on the east side of Commonwealth Avenue, bloom across the street from the Capitol's East Wing. In 1987 the General Assembly began occupancy of this impressive neo-classical wing that architecturally* links the 1906 Main Capitol with the North and South Office Buildings. ◉ **Bottom:** *George Barnard's sculpture, "Love and Labor: The Unbroken Law" shows human connectedness through meaningful work and loving family relationships. Situated on the south at the main entrance, these 1910 statues, which exude joy, camaraderie and forgiveness, are carved of Cararra marble from Italy.*

◉ **Top Left:** *The equestrian statue of General John Frederick Hartranft, Civil War hero and later governor, predates the present Capitol. Installed in front of the brick capitol in 1899, it was moved to its present stance facing south in front of the Capitol Annex Building in 1927.* ◉ **Bottom Left:** *Winter snow cloaks the still and silent fountain that is the focus of the spacious public* areas developed with the East Wing in the 1980s. ◉ **Above:** *"Commonwealth," a bronze and gilded 14' 6" high female statue by Roland Hinton Perry, has topped the Capitol Dome since 1905. Facing west, she balances on a gilt ball about 250 feet above street level. Her right arm extends in mercy while her other hand grasps a ribboned staff, a symbol of justice.*

⊠ *A winter moon accents the west and main facade of Pennsylvania's Capitol, an American Renaissance structure designed by Philadelphia architect Joseph M. Huston. This 52 million pound dome was inspired by St. Peter's Cathedral in Rome.*

ROTUNDA AND CORRIDOR ART

Visitors often pause in midstep as they enter the Capitol Rotunda. Its magnificence surprises them. Stunned by the lofty splendor, they often begin to whisper as if they had entered a cathedral.

Ahead, a white marble staircase gracefully sweeps upward to elegant triple arcades. Their linear symmetry pulls the eye from the floor to the lantern of the dome in one fluid motion. In that sweep, more than 200 feet high, vivid reds and blues gleam against gold surfaces.

For his Rotunda, architect Joseph Huston borrowed several design elements from the foyer of the Paris Opera House—the Neo-Baroque curves of the stairs, the arcaded gallery, and a marble banister on the second floor with metal railings on the upper levels. For the winged figures holding dazzling light spheres at the base of the stairway, the architect economized by substituting painted plaster figures for the more elaborate marble females in the Paris edifice.

Between the first and second floors, an entresol or intermediate floor, provides spaces for offices. Above its doorway, two putti, or cherubs, with dimpled buttocks hold an orb on a broken pediment, all of Vermont marble.

Ever since it was built, the Rotunda has been an arena for public events such as dedications and commemorations. Concerts, legislative photo opportunities and flag ceremonies also grace this richly decorated lobby.

It is a majestic setting for the Christmas trees that traditionally soar toward the dome each December. And on any day of the year, people pause and crane their necks to absorb the many details of this American Renaissance grandeur.

Along the upward swoop of the Rotunda are numerous neo-classical elements—caryatids or female figures serving as columns, gold-leafed capitals topping marble shafts, and griffins gaping from festoons. The design is enriched by rows of molding with motifs borrowed from the ancients—egg and dart, Greek key, acanthus leaf, and bead and reel. Bronze leafy vines wind around the light stands that rise out of the marble balustrade rimming the second floor.

The first floor of the Rotunda is also stunning. Wide Doric columns in threes line up to form vestibules that lead into the north and south corridors. Bronze fixtures on the first level support nine globes with scored glass that transforms each light bulb inside into a resplendent cross. Along the frieze near the ceiling are alternating images reminiscent of the decorations of Roman temples—concave circles and garlanded ox skulls or bucrane. The latter originated from the primitive practice of hanging an animal skull outside the temple where it was sacrificed.

Such a motif seems disparate in a gold leaf setting created by adhering small metallic squares of 22 carat gold to plaster or wood surfaces. The ceremonial doorways to the House and Senate are topped by heavily gilded reclining figures, reminiscent of the Medici tombs in Rome. Two bands of gold mosaic girdle the base of the dome and highlight a quotation by William Penn in blue letters: "There may be room for such a holy experiment. For the nations want a precedent. And my God will make it the seed of a nation. That an example may be set up to the nations. That we may do the thing that is truly wise and just."

Gold leaf is the background of the females adorning the medallions in the pendentives. Within these ovals are quotations found in an Egyptian temple and sayings from American nationalist Alexander Hamilton, the 16th century Protestant martyr Hugh Latimer, and the philosopher Plotinus. These medallions and the larger lunette murals in recessed arcs were painted between 1903 and 1907 by Edwin Austin Abbey (1852-1911), a Philadelphia artist of international renown.

Selecting Abbey as his first artist for the Capitol, the architect intended these paintings in the Rotunda to be the building's premier art pieces and discussed their themes in detail. Following Huston's visit to the artist's studio in Gloucestershire, England, Abbey remarked that the architect could give him more ideas in one day than he could paint in ten years.

Moreover, Abbey did extensive research before brushing any color on a canvas. It was customary for him to assemble many models in costume to make his mural scenes historically accurate. For the lunettes which combine spirits with Pennsylvania's industries, Abbey studied the nude form and pored over paintings of 17th century sailing vessels and photographs of oil derricks and production at Bethlehem Steel. He created colorful nymphs in classical garb overseeing work in mines, oil fields and steel mills. His imaginative murals are poetry on canvas–a visually appealing blend of toilsome production and spiritual guidance.

For the floor below, architect Huston decided on clay tiles produced by Mercer's Tileworks in Doylestown. In his pottery, archeologist Henry Chapman Mercer (1856-1930) had rekindled an ancient process that had been used to make the floor at St. Mark's in Venice. From Europe, Moravians had brought the technique to America, but it had vanished in Pennsylvania when Mercer began crafting ornamental tiles in 1898.

To fill his contract, by far his largest, Mercer provided thousands of handmade square tiles varying from rust to black as well as 377 tile mosaics depicting 254 subjects. At Huston's suggestion, Mercer developed picture tiles resembling German woodcuts. From the staircase in the Rotunda, these intermittent image tiles relieve the continuous sea of burnished rust. Huston, who had originally planned for marble mosaics, must have been pleased that Mercer's choice of subjects expanded the architect's original themes by adding natural history and Native American lifeways to the Capitol art.

In the Preface to his 1908 guidebook to the tiled floor, Mercer wrote, "It is the life of the people that is sought to be expressed; the building of a commonwealth economically great, by the individual work of thousands of hands, rather than by wars and legislatures."

Mercer's Capitol mosaics reflect his idealization of handtooled artifacts. Beginning chronologically in the north transverse wing, these tiles dot the expanse of the floor, illustrating Native American crafts, early European settler skills and, in the South Wing, the inventions of the industrial age. Sprinkled throughout are the state's native flora and fauna, such as a wolf, a turtle and a butterfly.

The murals of the South Corridor were executed by William B. Van Ingen (1858-1955), a Philadelphian who was also accomplished at stained glass art. In the South Corridor of the first floor, Van Ingen chose to paint the most noble characteristic of Penn's colony–its toleration of all religions compatible with monotheism. Van Ingen's 14 murals feature what he considered to be key events and practices of Pennsylvania's numerous sects. Their tone is cool and earthy. Nature is quietly present, but the world of the inner spirit dominates. Some of the murals illustrate such historical happenings as the printing of the Bible by Christopher Sauer; the arrival of Quakers and Mennonites to Germantown in the late 17th century; and the Scotch Irish founding of Log College, a Presbyterian predecessor of Princeton University. Several of these moon-shaped lunettes depict practices of various sects–Dunkards baptizing in a stream, Quaker women sitting in silent worship in a meetinghouse and a Moravian woman teaching two Native Americans to read.

Generally, Van Ingen saluted ethnic history accurately. For example, the German Mennonites who settled in Pennsylvania did not practice the ritual of washing feet. Consequently, the sisters washing feet in Van Ingen's mural are dressed in the garb of Dutch, not German, Mennonites. However, the artist did depict one image that cannot be historically documented. Although printed in a "Ripley's Believe It Or Not" column in the 1930s, it is a myth that Peter Mueller (Miller), a leader and printer among the Ephrata Brethren, transcribed the Declaration of Independence into seven languages for Congress, as one Van Ingen lunette portrays.

For many years the lunettes along the corridor on the other side of the Rotunda were vacant. Despite a 1911 appropriation to commission art for the North Corridor, it was not until the early 70s that Vincent Maragliotti (1888-1978) painted 14 canvases featuring the state's industrial and mechanical development. The scenes document, among other trades, steel manufacturing, road building and farm production.

Female figures representing the four seasons gain the attention of visitors approaching the main corridors from the far entrances on the west facade. A skilled artisan, Donald R. MacGregor (1870-1930) no doubt painted these allegorical images on the spandrels of the arches above the light courts–"Spring" and "Summer" in the South Corridor and "Autumn" and "Winter" in the North. The Philadelphia firm, D.A. MacGregor & Bro. was commissioned to do all of the Capitol decorating. Aiming to enhance the architecture, MacGregor probably added the stenciling surrounding his figures.

The same purpose motivated the carving of portrait heads decorating the capitals of pilasters in the first-floor corridors. Each is a specific individual representing an ethnic group that helped to found Pennsylvania. Foliage of a plant symbolizes the person's background. For instance, a tulip suggests David Rittenhouse's Dutch origins, and a rose near Daniel Boone connotes his English heritage.

To this day, because of financial constraints, some of the sculpture niches where Huston had planned to install classical figures remain barren. However, from the start the Commission supported installing fine art on the walls of the Governor's Reception Room, where the governor of the Keystone State receives visitors.

Huston's decision to commission a female, Philadelphia artist Violet Oakley (1874-1961), to paint this spacious anteroom created headlines. He chose her because he believed that her themes reflected a deep "religious, philosophical strain." Also, he wanted her selection "to act as an encouragement of women of the State." Oakley's strong convictions persuaded Huston and the Commission to accept her plans illustrating the events of Penn's life and his society as the foundation of religious liberty that gave birth to

Pennsylvania. Oakley believed that these influences were more pivotal in the creation of Pennsylvania than such happenings as Penn's peaceful agreements with the Indians.

The 13 panels titled, "The Founding of the 'State of Liberty Spiritual,'" cover a century before Penn and chronicle the martyrdom of the English Bible translator William Tyndale in 1536 and, a decade later, of Anna Askew, the great grandmother of Margaret Fell, the wife of the founder of the Quakers, George Fox. Oakley felt that these events helped to inspire Penn's creation of a haven of spiritu-al liberty. However, her paintings also raised the ire of some Pennsylvania Catholics who resented having their persecution of Protestants illustrated so publicly.

Fortunately, the ruckus settled and Oakley proceeded painting at Cogslea, an estate near Philadelphia with studio space and gardens for her and her friends who were also accomplished artists. Working from a scaffolding, Oakley filled canvases six feet high and at least 11 feet long with scenes depicting Penn's life in England. After the panels were hung in 1906, Pennsylvanians could see their founder studying at Oxford, inspired by the peace-loving Quaker mystic George Fox, denounced by his admiral father for his Quaker sympathies , arrested and then imprisoned. The last scene shows Penn aboard ship anticipating his arrival to create a "Holy Experiment." A Christian Scientist with a deep admiration for Quaker ideals, Oakley later painstakingly prepared portfolios of her series in order to explain the moral timbre of her murals.

Each year, thousands of visitors step into the awesome beauty of the Rotunda, its connecting corridors and the Governor's Reception Room. They can gain inspiration from the fine and decorative arts created by the talents of Huston, Abbey, Van Ingen and other artists. The architecture as well as the paintings, statuary and finishes that adorn these public spaces remains an artistic treasure in Pennsylvania.

◙ **Previous pages:** *Gold leaf, white marble and glittering crystal combine to create a magnificent Rotunda which rises 272 feet to the colorful roof of the dome.* ◙ **Above:** *Edwin A. Abbey painted the four lunettes and four medallions in the Rotunda. The murals are esteemed for their blending of allegory and realism. "The Spirit of Religious Liberty" accompanies the feminine spirits of Faith and Hope in guiding ships to Pennsylvania, a religious haven for settlers. In the circular paintings, females symbolize Science and Art with quotations from both the Egyptian Temple of Isis and the second century philosopher Plotinus.*

The subject of "The Spirit of Light" by Abbey implies that Pennsylvania sheds light in the world in two regards–physically, via derricks that pump oil from the earth and spiritually, through the message of Founder William Penn. His memorable words citing Pennsylvania as "a holy experiment" with God making it "the seed of a nation" are written in blue letters on the mosaic gold frieze that encircles the Rotunda above and below the pendentives. Between them are two medallions honoring Art and Law; the latter portrays a female whose blindfold suggests that justice should be blind.

◈ *"Science Revealing the Treasures of the Earth," a lunette mural by Abbey, hangs on the west wall of the Rotunda. Science, the central winged maiden, guides miners in their conquest of the Commonwealth's natural resources. Science's burnished wings have the same tone as the red earth. The medallions of Law and Religion flank this mural; the latter features a quotation of Hugh Latimer, sixteenth century English bishop and martyr.*

THE SPIRIT OF VULCAN

◙ *"The Spirit of Vulcan" developed from Abbey's imagination and his study of Bethlehem Steel machinery. In this oil painting, the strong-limbed god Vulcan oversees the demanding labor of steelworkers and smiths in the ruby glow of the smelting furnace. After these murals of 38 x 22 feet were installed in 1908, critics agreed that they gave people a sense of what Pennsylvania owes to divine inspiration and the earth's abundance.*

■ *Left: To greet people entering the wide and beautifully decorated Rotunda, architect Joseph Huston designed a sweeping marble staircase that resembles the one in the Paris Opera House.* ■ *Above: The ceiling of the Dome is a symmetrical blend of gold, red and blue. Arabesques of Rennaissance ornament fill the space between the 16 ribs.*

◈ **Above:** Rich in classical ornamental detail, the restored north light court leads into the corridor that is lit by pumpkin ball chandeliers. The allegorical maidens, Autumn and Winter, which decorate the spandrels of the arches, were painted by a skilled artisan. On the beam are Doric symbols– triglyphs, or vertical grooves, alternating with ox-skulls and circles. ◈ **Right:** Spring and Summer, figures in "The Four Seasons" which was painted by the Philadelphia decorating firm, D.A. MacGregor & Bro., adorn the south light court that leads to arcaded balconies above the first floor.

◉ *Left: A corridor extending from the Rotunda is divided into bays by a series of pilasters. These attached columns are topped with gilded capitals of portrait heads of Pennsylvanians representing the ethnic groups that settled the colony.* ◉ *Above left: The floor of the first level is reddish tile pavement that was fired at Moravian Tileworks in Doylestown. Its owner, Henry C. Mercer,* designed mosaic picture tiles featuring the life of Pennsylvania's inhabitants, including animal creatures. Mercer even devoted one of his 377 mosaics to the lowly house fly.
◉ *Above right: Mercer's "Paring Apples" illustrates the use of a mechanical device that peeled apples for cider in Pennsylvania up to 1860.*

■ *Left: Among his many tiles of Indian arti-facts, Mercer included this Indian drawing of a spider that had been scratched on a shell.* ■ **Above:** *In the 1970s, for the north corridor of the Capitol, Vincent Maragliotti painted 14 lunettes that show Pennsylvanians at work. Among several paintings of indus-tries on the west wall, the above mural illustrates mining.*

■ *Above: William B. Van Ingen painted lunettes illustrating events and practices among the sects that came to Pennsylvania for religious freedom. Daniel Pastorius, leader of Mennonite and Quaker immigrants to Germantown, circulates the first protest against slavery in 1683. (left) A Sauer press prints the Bible for early colonists.* ■ *Right: On the west wall of the Capitol Rotunda's north corridor, "Amish Farming 1730-1740" leads the Vincent Maragliotti series on Pennsylvania industries.*

■ **Above:** *Although most of Van Ingen's paintings are based on documented history, this mural of Peter Miller, one of the Ephrata Brethren, translating the Declaration of Independence into seven languages for the early Congress cannot be substantiated. To the right hangs a lunette showing the landing of the boat "Concord" with the first settlers of Germantown, Philadelphia.*

■ **Right:** *Van Ingen's cool, pastoral images line the first floor corridor south of the Rotunda. The above lunette portrays William Tenant, Sr., Scotch Irish professor, teaching ministerial candidates at Log College near the fork of the Neshaminy Creek, Bucks County, Pennsylvania. This institution was the predecessor of Princeton University, New Jersey.*

■ **Above:** *Furnishings of carved oak and gilded leather decorate the Governor's Reception Room on the second floor. The room's inscribed paintings titled "The Founding of the 'State of Liberty Spiritual'" were completed in 1906 by Violet Oakley, the first woman artist to receive a major public art commission in America.* ■ **Top Right:** *Oakley's murals show the life and times of William Penn, Pennsylvania's founder. One of the 16 panels portrays Admiral Penn's rejection of his son's decision to follow the peace-loving, persecuted Quakers. Young William receives a comforting lick from their family dog. The same species, the Great Dane, is Pennsylvania's state dog.* ■ **Right:** *The above segment of a 6' x 19' mural illustrates the condemnation of Penn for violation of the Conventicle Acts, which forbade any worship service except that of the Church of England. While in Newgate Prison, according to the next panel, Penn wrote about the liberty of conscience and envisioned his Holy Experiment.*

ADMIRAL PENN·DENOUNCING·AND·TURNING·HIM·FROM·HOME·BECAUSE·OF·
HIS·SYMPATHY·WITH·THE·DESPISED·SECT·OF·QUAKERS·····
"FORGET·ALSO·THINE·OWN·PEOPLE·AND·THY·FATHERS·HOUSE"

···· PREACHING·AT·OXFORD ···
····· WILL·POUR·ON·ALL·FLESH··YOUR
····· ····· SHALL·SEE·VISIONS

WRITING·IN·PRISON·····THE·GREAT·CASE·OF·
LIBERTY·OF·CONSCIENCE·ONCE·MORE·BRIEFLY
DEBATED·AND·DEFENDED"

THAT·ARE·AFFLICTED·FOR·IT···· PENN·EXAMIN
BY·THE·LIEUTENANT·OF·THE·TOWER·OF·LON·
CONDEMNED·TO·IMPRISONMENT·IN·NEWGATE

SENATE CHAMBER

rchitect Joseph M. Huston hoped the Senate Chamber would be one of the "most beautiful colored rooms in this country." Green and gold combine majestically in this 96 x 80 foot room on the second floor of the north arm of the Capitol. The brilliance increases with the gold near the ceilings and in the balconies where visitors sit.

From this gallery, one sees the mahogany desks of Pennsylvania's 50 Senators. Elected for four-year terms, these legislators sit in ten rows of five, facing the rostrum to debate and vote on bills. Only Senators and staff occupy the floor. Media people stay behind a brass rail in this legislative chamber.

However, all can view this Chamber's distinctive French Renaissance decor. Along the walls the wainscot of Irish Green Connemara marble is more beautiful because horizontal veins of green and beige flow in waves. Workmen installed thin marble slices that had been cut vertically. The visual effect of the cross-section simulates an undulating grassy plain.

Gold dominates the ceiling where six massive chandeliers hang from the intersection of beams. Gold acanthus leaves, a Mediterranean species first copied by Greek architects, gleam from the breast of the beams. Recessed coffers with classical motifs and ornate rosettes in the center illustrate the detailed planning of the architect, who found inspiration for this room in the Cathedral of Saint John Lateran in Rome.

Although the Chamber was used from 1906 when the building was dedicated, its murals were not installed until 1917. Following the unexpected death of the commissioned artist, E.A. Abbey, in 1911, the Commission asked Violet Oakley, muralist for the Governor's Reception Room, to produce the paintings for this Chamber.

Oakley, who relished history as a story that unfolded on the pages of time, reveled in interpreting its events on canvas. She chose to base the realistic mural cycle in the Senate Chamber on Pennsylvania's role in the story of America's nationhood, giving it the title, "The Creation and Preservation of the Union." She designed pairs of panels on each of the following subjects: United States presidents in moments of decisive leadership; episodes from two cataclysmic wars on American soil; and on an allegorical level, two representations of the enemies of unity and two scenes from folklore illustrating victory over slavery and war.

But the most striking image among the nine panels in this room is Unity, a female figure dominating a 40 foot long central mural. This blue-robed woman, dripping with the "pure river of water of life" presides over the end of warfare and slavery. Oakley painted the social ideals that she longed for. She worked for them when she joined the Women's League for Peace and Freedom, an organization founded by her friend, Jane Addams, during World War I. Oakley ardently supported the League of Nations as an effort to unite against further international war. She foresaw that it could return governments to the path that Penn had charted.

This "modest, capable, splendid Pennsylvania woman," as Governor Martin G. Brumbaugh described Oakley, enjoyed linking the past to her vision of an ideal future. During the unveiling, Oakley endearingly called Unity, her woman in blue, a source of purity, life and the wisdom of love. Oakley's female figure is strong, trustworthy and giving but without cherubic passivity or sensuous passion. In the crystal clear water that flows from and around Unity, diverse people find peace. Their weapons are cleansed and their children restored.

This theme, hinging on images in the Book of Revelation in the Bible, developed as Oakley described the impact of her research: "A profound wonder overwhelmed me as I learned more and more of the great, positive constructive principle informing the founder of Pennsylvania's first government." Still reeling from the devastation of World War I, she admired the Quaker ideal of representative government for citizens enjoying freedom of religion and absence of differing rank. She called this pure democracy a miracle, truly a Holy Experiment. And she hoped that her paintings would inspire government to be its best, "a thing sacred" by "crushing the effects of evil" and giving people security.

Two lunettes of the Senate Chamber frieze show the violence of war and slavery, evils that would be washed away by the power of Unity. This subject becomes more concrete in the two panels on the south wall that portray legendary tales of good triumphing over evil. In "The Sanctuary In the Wilderness" a peace-loving Quaker couple living on the frontier were startled one night by Indians who merely opened the door and then departed without doing harm. Earlier the settlers had betrayed their usual practice of keeping the leather latchstring outside in welcome. However, unable to sleep, they had arisen and put out the latchstring again believing they

would be safe "in the keeping of the Omnipotent Spirit."

Later, at a conference with the Indians during peaceful times, the Friend related this experience and an Indian confessed that he was among the marauding braves. He related that putting out the latchstring, a simple act showing confidence rather than fear, had spared the Friends' lives. "We saw that with the door unbarred, you trusted the Great Spirit." Oakley pictures this spiritual safety with an angel protecting the settlers. Below, five small panels with inscriptions illustrate Christ's death and resurrection.

The other legend painted under

a bay balcony shows Quakers purchasing a whole shipload of slaves with the intention of freeing them. There is no precise documentation on this although many American Quakers were known to free slaves, sometimes ingeniously. Four smaller scenes underneath depict experiences from the journal of John Woolman, a Quaker who protested human slavery.

The distinction of Oakley's Capitol commission was not lost on her relatives, several of whom were also artists. Within the scrapbook her mother kept on her daughter's career is an untitled and undated news clip-

ping that reads, "For the first time in American history a woman is to be entrusted with the mural decoration of a great public building."

Oakley was not the only artist who contributed to the Chamber's beauty. At a lofty height, direct light from the east and west filters through 10 round stained glass windows. Each one depicts a human figure symbolizing one of the arts or sciences that propelled Pennsylvania's development forward. Architecture, History, Temperance, Legislature and Peace are included as well as Foundries, Railroads, Glass Blowing, Weaving and Militia.

Artist William B. Van Ingen designed these rounds, planning the colorful tones and lead glazing of each figure. His vibrant blues and greens harmonize with the decor.

Van Ingen studied the production of opalescent glass under Louis C. Tiffany and John LaFarge, who patented the technique. Four layers of painted glass help create iridescense when sunlight shines through. Although still, the color seems to quiver, the shading mirroring depth as seen in the texture of a fold in a sleeve or the strength of a reaching arm.

At the end of the workday in winter, the setting sun lights Van Ingen's stained glass with a luminous intensity that further tints the room known as the Green Room by the Senators. The gifts and visions of both Van Ingen and Oakley combine to make the Senate Chamber an inspiration.

Left: *Violet Oakley 's mural on the north wall of the Senate Chamber shows George Washington presiding at the Constitutional Convention in May 1787 with the Pennsylvania delegation surrounding him. Realism reigns in the details–the stoop of an aged Ben Franklin, the design of the column and its pedestal, and the high-backed chair with its famous rising sun carving. And how closely the inkstand on the desk resembles the one designed by Philip Syng and used by the framers to sign the Constitution! Each of the faces is recognizable; however, Oakley painted only the back of the head of Thomas Fitzsimmons because there is no known portrait of this delegate.*

The presence of a black man in a servantile position connotes a reminder by the artist that not all citizens were included in the Bill of Rights being discussed at the Convention.

Above: *Foliated bronze scrolling over the barrel vault ceiling provides a rich setting for William B. Van Ingen's ten stained glass windows. Located on the east and west walls, their iridescent colors glow in the rising and setting sunlight. The maidens symbolize (l. to r.) Weaving, Temperance, Glass Blowing and Peace.*

⊗ *Previous pages: Green and gold blend in the Senate Chamber, a spacious 95 feet in width. Irish Connemara marble wainscot, coffered green ceilings and gilded bronze complete the color scheme while Violet Oakley's murals present historical and allegorical subjects.* ⊗ *Above: In Van Ingen's windows, beautifully garbed females and appropriate emblems represent the arts and sciences, here (l. to r.) Legislature, History, Foundries and Architecture. **Right:** Within Oakley's mural cycle, "The Creation and Preservation of the Union," the right-hand arched panel shows a very sad President Abe Lincoln giving his famous Gettysburg Address in November 1863.*

◙ *Top Left: "Militia" is the title of a stained glass window in which two emblems, "a bayonet representing its military purpose and a keystone its civic aspect," are pictured with a maiden.* ◙ *Left: Classical motifs in the moldings and scrollwork enhance Van Ingen's recessed stained glass windows.*

◙ *Top: Gilded embossed ornamentation above the windows is reminiscent of designs in St. John Lateran, a church in Rome.* ◙ *Above: A stained glass window named "Railroads" represents one of Pennsylvania's industries. Brilliance and graceful composition characterize these restored opalescent windows.*

WASHINGTON · MARCHING · THROUGH · PHILADELPHIA · 1777
GOING · DOWN · TO · THE · BRANDYWINE

"IT · WAS · NOT · THE · MERE · MATTER · OF · SEPARATION · OF · THE · COLONIES · FROM · THE · MOTHERLAND · BUT · THAT · SENTIMENT · IN · THE · DECLARATION · OF · INDEPENDENCE · WHICH · GAVE · LIBERTY · NOT · ALONE · TO · THIS · COUNTRY · BUT · HOPE · TO · ALL · THE · WORLD · FOR · ALL · FUTURE · TIME."

GENERAL · MEADE · AND · PENNSYLVANIA · TROOPS
IN · CAMP · BEFORE · GETTYSBURG

"IT · WAS · THAT · WHICH · GAVE · PROMISE · THAT · IN · DUE · TIME · THE · WEIGHTS · WOULD · BE · LIFTED · FROM · THE · SHOULDERS · OF · ALL · MEN · AND · THAT · ALL · SHOULD · HAVE · AN · EQUAL · CHANCE"
FROM · ABRAHAM · LINCOLN'S · ADDRESS · IN · INDEPENDENCE · HALL · FEBRUARY · 22nd 1861

◈ *Above:* *Oakley murals hang above doorways along the north wall of the Chamber where the Commonwealth's 50 Senators convene. They show troop movement–(top) George Washington's revolutionaries on their way to the Battle of Brandywine and (below) General George Meade's Union men departing from Camp Curtin in Harrisburg en route to Gettysburg.* ◈ **Top Right:** *An extensive* allegorical frieze near the ceiling includes a demi-lune depicting "The Slaves of the Earth Driven Forward and Upward by Their Slavedrivers, Greed and Ignorance and Fear."
◈ **Right:** "The Armies of the Earth Striving Together to Take the Kingdom of Unity by Violence" is the left demi-lune by Violet Oakley, a talented artist and social activist who put her peaceful ideals on canvas.

THEY DID SET OVER
THEM TASK MASTERS
TO AFFLICT THEM
WITH THEIR BURDENS
AND THEY MADE THEY
LIVES BITTER THEY
... HAVE SEEN THE AFFLICTION OF MY

THE KINGDOM
OF UNITED
SUFFERETH
VIOLENCE AND
THE VIOLENT
WOULD TAKE
IT BY FORCE

Introduced with a border that reads, "Here beginneth the Legend of Peace," the mural "The Sanctuary in the Wilderness" hangs on the Senate Chamber's south wall. In this Quaker legend, war-whooping tribesmen spared a frontier couple because the settlers had placed trust in the Great Spirit by leaving the leather thong that controlled the bar of their door outside–a gesture of welcome. A woman ahead of her times, Oakley supported multi-ethnicity with details in this cabin scene.

In the south wall mural titled "The Slave Ship Ransomed," plainly dressed Quakers have boarded a slave ship about to land and have purchased its enire load of human cargo. According to the legend, the abolitionists then headed north to Nova Scotia to set the slaves free. Oakley illustrated this legend to inspire justice. In five small paintings in the predella below, the artist presents Jesus of the Bible liberating the imprisoned from Hell and aspects of the life of the American Quaker John Woolman, whose 18th century journal recounts his beliefs and efforts to defeat slavery.

▣ *The central panel of the frieze above the Speaker's Rostrum, "International Understanding and Unity" shows Unity, a utopian woman dressed in the blue healing waters of life. She lovingly unites people of all races and ages, thus erasing differences that cause wars. Oakley believed that government as Penn had envisoned it, could rule and reach "the beauty of Unity."*

SUPREME AND SUPERIOR COURT ROOM

he Supreme Court of Pennsylvania is the oldest court in North America. Its establishment in 1722 was essentially a renaming of the Provincial Court which had been handing decisions down since 1684. In these early years of Penn's colony, judicial proceedings were secondary to the guarantee of liberties.

The early Court, in fact, did not have a home. Its sessions were first conducted in private Philadelphia houses. Later it met in the State House (now Independence Hall) until 1790. The Court established a district in Harrisburg in 1807 shortly before this city became the state's seat of government.

Today, the Supreme Court consists of seven justices elected to serve a set ten-year term. The jurisdiction of the Pennsylvania Supreme Court is much wider today than at its inception when the chief justice and two associates held semi-annual sessions in Philadelphia and rode circuit on horseback the rest of the year. Circuit duties stopped when districts were set up in 1809.

Demand grew so that in 1895 the Superior Court was established to lighten the burden of the Supreme Court.

Located on the Capitol's fourth floor, the Supreme Court Chamber heralds "interior decorations of a high order," as planned by architect Joseph Huston. In this room, paired Ionic pilasters or attached columns separate Violet Oakley's rich gold and orange-toned murals. A classical Greek grille makes up the walls of Honduran mahogany and the shallow drum of the central dome. The major ornamental feature of the room is a hemispheric stained glass dome with a foliated anthemion motif, a classical design element based on the flower and leaves of the honeysuckle. William B. Van Ingen designed this skylight of stained glass. Egg and dart mouldings carry out the neo-classical design with restraint.

It was important to artist Violet Oakley that the message of her murals would not "dwarf the importance of the living law going on within its walls." Titled "The Opening of the Book of the Law," these murals scroll out the development of law through the ages. In this her third and last commission for the Capitol, Oakley blended extensive text with symbolic design and figures. The 16 finished works resemble, in Oakley's own words, "the illuminations of ancient manuscripts."

Interestingly enough, Oakley organized the cycle of paintings according to the musical scale. Divine Law, the first and last note, graces the main entrance to the court room. She traces contributions of nature, the Greeks, the Hebrews and the Romans as well as such individuals as William Penn, William Blackstone and John Marshall. Her idealism surfaces through her concluding themes of peace overcoming evil and law purifying and enlightening countries. Her images end in a crescendo of hope with Divine Law an octave higher to symbolize progress towards peace. Malcolm Vaughn of the *New York Herald-Tribune* credited her with "raising an international altar to the Victory of Law over Force."

Oakley's murals, Van Ingen's stained glass dome and Honduran mahogany fittings unite to create a room of exquisite beauty. The setting provides a home for the highest Court in Pennsylvania and the oldest appellate court in the nation.

Within the mural image:

COPYRIGHT 1920
By VIOLET OAKLEY

Thou shalt have No Other Gods before Me.
Thou shalt not make unto Thee Any Graven Image: *thou shalt not bow down thyself to them nor serve them.*
Thou shalt not take the Name of the LORD Thy GOD in vain
Remember the Sabbath DAY to Keep it holy. Honour Thy Father and Thy Mother

Thou shalt not Kill. Thou shalt not commit adultery. Thou shalt not steal. Thou shalt not bear false Witness... Thou shalt Not covet Thy Neighbor's house. Thou shalt not covet Thy Neighbor's Wife nor his Manservant, nor his Maidservant, nor his Ox, nor his Ass, nor anything that is his.

MOSAIC · DECALOGUE

Above: *Violet Oakley painted murals that were placed above the mahogany wainscot. Each of the 16 wall panels resembles a page in an illuminated manuscript. With words and images inside richly colored borders, the murals recount the development of law from the beginning of time up to a utopian future. The Ten Commandments or Decalogue was a contribution of the Hebrews.* **Right:** *In the Supreme Court Room ceiling, a stained glass dome by Pennsylvania artist William B. Van Ingen glows green and yellow.*

REVEAL: ED LAW

Blessed are the poor in Spirit:
for theirs is the kingdom of heaven.

Blessed are they that mourn: for
they shall be comforted.

Blessed are the meek: for they
shall inherit the Earth.

Blessed are they which do hunger
and thirst after righteousness:
for they shall be filled.

Blessed are the merciful: for they
shall obtain Mercy.

Blessed are the Pure in heart:
for they shall see God.

Blessed are the Peace-makers: for
they shall be called the Children
of God.

Blessed are they which are persecuted
for righteousness' sake: for theirs is
the kingdom of heaven.

Blessed are ye when men shall revile
you and persecute you and shall say all
manner of evil against you falsely for
my sake. Rejoice, and be exceeding glad, for
great is your reward in heaven:
for so persecuted they the
prophets which were before you.

LAW OF ✠ REASON

CAESAR I was and am JUSTINIAN. "By Will of the Divine LOVE I drew out from among the LAWS the Superfluous and the Vain." [Prochium to Digest Cased VI, 1] Man considered as a CREATURE must be subject to the Laws of his CREATOR for he is an entirely dependent being. The CREATOR being of INFINITE POWER and also of INFINITE WISDOM has laid down only such Laws as were found in their relation to JUSTICE that existed in the Nature of things antecedent to any Positive Precept. Such are these PRINCIPLES: "That we should live honestly." That we should hurt Nobody. And should render to Everyone his due. To which general Precept JUSTINIAN has reduced The Whole DOCTRINE of LAW." Blackstone

CODE OF ✠ JUSTINIAN

Previous pages: *Oakley included The Beatitudes, which recommend forgiveness and mercy, as the thesis of Christendom. Oakley said that Roman Law purported justice, discarding "the superfluous and the vain" and supported "rendering to others what is due, living honestly and not hurting anybody."* **Above:** *Oakley symbolically pictured the Law of Nature (left panel) and Greek law as developed by Themis. (right)* **Top Right:** *"William Penn as Law-Giver" recognizes Penn's plan for a Parliament of Nations which was advanced thinking*

for the 17th century. (left) A panel featuring The Supreme Court of Pennsylvania lauds James Wilson, a justice who ably interpreted the Constitution here in the land expansion case of Republica vs. de Longchamps in 1784. Chief Justice Thomas McKean is presiding . **Right:** *The final mural page depicts Christ walking on the agitated waters of the world and sinking battleships–Oakley's vote for disarmament. A detail of this panel portrays a strong being with both male and female characteristics.*

▨ **Left:** *Organizing the cycle as a musical scale, the artist called Divine Law the Keynote. Oakley created a monogram with the letters L, A and W intertwining, and then, like a puzzlegram, forming the words Love, And and Wisdom.* ▨ **Above:** *"The Spirit of Law–Purification and Enlightenment"*

finishes the series. A listing of seven kinds of law in the order they appear completes the octave in The Scale of Law and serves as the cycle's Table of Contents. A barefoot harpist gracefully plays in the center of the first letter of the title, T.

HOUSE OF REPRESENTATIVES CHAMBER

Since its beginnings in the seventeenth century, Pennsylvania's House of Representatives has embodied democratic representation. Founder William Penn envisioned a colony with a broad participatory government. Although it did not develop to match his ideal, the system that emerged gave birth to America's first independent legislative body.

In 1692 at Chester, Penn convened a 42-member Colonial Assembly that was the forerunner of the state's legislature. Today, after more than three centuries as a continuing organization, the House totals 203 legislators who are elected every two years by the citizens within their geographic districts. While in session, members gather in the House Chamber, one of the most significant rooms in the Capitol.

In this room Pennsylvanians have a voice. The sovereignty of the people is symbolized by the mace, a solid mahogany staff capped by a brass globe with the state's coat of arms attached. An American eagle perches on top. A tradition of authority that preserves peace and order, the mace harks back to Roman rulers. Now it accompanies the Speaker of the House during each session day and remains at the right of the rostrum until the House recesses or adjourns. In both the Senate and the House, the mace is a concrete reminder that those governing are also governed.

The importance of representative government for the first colonial settlers who sailed up the Delaware grew as democratic representation became a goal of the 13 colonies in their revolutionary endeavor to form a nation. Other political contributions the House spawned for the United States of America were the two-party system, the member-selected Speaker, taxation only by representative vote and legislative authority over government spending. The House utilized its legislative powers to create a Supreme Court in 1722 and the office of elected governor in 1790.

In addition to its remarkable record of governmental achievements, the House of Representatives serves in a resplendent chamber noted for its art. Blue and gold dominate an Italian Renaissance decor with art by William B. Van Ingen and Edwin A. Abbey.

When Pennsylvania native Edwin Abbey received a list for possible historic scenes for the legislative chambers, he resisted these suggestions prepared by history buff Governor Samuel Pennypacker, declining to paint realistic textbook panels of Pennsylvania's past. Abbey wrote from his English residence that he would combine several subjects into larger presentations. Even though he was being paid per square foot, he agreed to provide the larger paintings at no additional fee out of his desire "to satisfy his own sense of artistic achievement, and thus give the Commonwealth the very best work he is capable of producing."

In fact, in 1906 Abbey requested that the diameter of the circular ceiling panel be enlarged from 18 to 24 feet. Architect Huston accommodated his request, altering a heavy molding planned for the circumference. In this star-studded mural, "The Hours," Abbey created a passage-of-time fantasy with each of 24 female figures representing an hour of the day. Peeking from the dark cloak of night, a maiden hesitantly greets the dawn. Each female emerges more fully with the progression of the hours.

As midday approaches, she engages in life energetically and in the brightness of noon, dances with vigor. The joined hands of the damsels symbolize the continuum of time. The artist shows more color in each maiden's diaphanous garb as the intensity of noon wanes throughout the afternoon into the orange-red glow of dusk. The night's blackness slowly shrouds the human form with the face being the last to drop into concealment. Moonrise and brighter stars surround the obscured human form at midnight.

In the very center of "The Hours," constellations including the Milky Way fill the circular heavens painted with a range of blues. To retain their luminosity, Abbey mixed his paint with wax. Over the years this binding element caused the flaking and loss of pigment discovered by the chief conservator in 1988 when the murals were cleaned. At the same time it was observed that paint drips on this massive round ran in a concentric pattern, an indication that Abbey might have worked with this canvas on a rotating vertical easel.

In order to harmonize with the ceiling mural, Abbey proposed blue and and cream ornamentation for the House, honoring the architect's wish "to have the harmony of your pictures and walls in unit,..." Deep blue walls contrast with a wainscoting of cream marble with hints of rose and gray. This supposedly originated from a quarry owned by priests in the French Pyrenees, but to this day, the source of the marble in the House Chamber is still being researched.

The trios of Corinthian columns above this marble base are plaster with gilded capitals. Above them, an elaborate architrave includes a frieze with gold honeysuckle against a blue band that anticipates the barrel vault ceiling in the same color. This arched roof is punctuated by circular stained glass windows that become lambent in intense sunlight.

The commission of these 14 glass rounds, each with a central human figure, was completed by William B. Van Ingen, a superb colorist. Each human is pictured with an object denoting one of the areas of social and scientific development. Most of the symbolic figures are female, but the one representing Steel is male. The clothing of the fig-

ures is no less than exquisite. Shading details in the gowns worn by Commerce, Petroleum, Bridge Building and Justice emphasize the best translucence of the stained glass. Education, Liberty and Religion rank alongside more concrete emblems such as Steam Engine, Printing Press, Electricity and Natural Gas. It was Van Ingen's study under John LaFarge and Louis Tiffany that led an artist so thoroughly comfortable with murals to master both the placement and painting of glass pieces to create another type of art.

None of Van Ingen's Capitol contributions come close in popularity to the Abbey mural, "The Camp of the American Army at Valley Forge," which hangs alone beside blank panels on the rear wall of House Chamber. Originally painted for the Senate, it was moved here when Oakley took on the commission for the smaller chamber.

With historical authenticity, Abbey painted his interpretation of training during a Valley Forge encampment in the Revolutionary War. His work portrays the Prussian "Baron" Friedrich von Steuben forcefully drilling a regiment of tattered patriots on a snowy field. The painting, well-loved across the nation, exemplifies the sacrifice made in Pennsylvania for political independence. Visitors relish the opportunity to view this heritage masterpiece closeup.

Two larger murals, also realistic, flank the Chamber's centerpiece on the south wall. "Penn's Treaty with the Indians" and "The Reading of the Declaration of Independence," illustrating two significant happenings on Pennsylvania soil, fill the space above the pediments of two double doors. Penn's appearance at 42 years of age, complete with his blue waistsash, offers a more realistic portrayal of this event than the one by artist Benjamin West in the 18th century.

Abbey postponed finishing the second painting in hopes of finding a rendering of the Rittenhouse Observatory from which Colonel John Nixon read the Declaration of Independence. After Abbey's unexpected death, one of his assistants, Ernest Board, painted the final details, placing Colonel Nixon on a white balcony, as suggested by Abbey's artist friend, John Singer Sargent. The location of the Observatory and its wooden platform was discovered just before Abbey's death.

The ceiling is striking, especially when viewed from the balconies. Rosettes in recessed squares line the beams of richly embellished coffers. Foliated bronze scrolls across blue ceiling sections. Six heavily gilt chandeliers resemble bouquets, but these are lit with a total of 1,003 light bulbs. Each large candelabra reportedly weighs four tons and hangs from a structural beam. The chandeliers' sumptuous Renaissance details are almost beyond the imagination.

From the visitor balconies, Abbey's stately masterpiece, "The Apotheosis" immediately lures a viewer into its fullness. The title of this 35 foot square mural means "the perfect example." The largest piece of art in the Capitol, it is a painting of 35 famous Pennsylvanians assembled on temple steps ascending to a statue of the Goddess of Genius. Because its perspective reaches to each corner of the wall rather than stopping within the confines of a molding frame, "Apotheosis" resembles a stage set. Abbey had waited over four years for permission to extend it down to the wainscot.

Painting this enormous scene became a major production with props, mannequins, live models, oil sketches and assistants all playing a role at Abbey's bidding. He used varying tones to distinguish allegory from realism in this scene.

In this imaginative mural, the goddess figure sitting in the cupola of the picture, represents the inspiring guidance of the ideal, the Commonwealth. The first level of distinguished men includes early explorers and navigators Peter Minuit, Henrik Hudson and Sir Walter Raleigh, people who arrived on North American soil too early to be called Pennsylvanians. To their right stand the trailblazers on land–pioneer Daniel Boone, colony organizer Daniel Pastorius and the mystic Kelpius.

The next lower level features Pennsylvanians of the cloth and of the law who are seated and fearless patriots such as "Mad" Anthony Wayne, who is drawing his sword. Among other builders of a developing society are astronomer David Rittenhouse in a green vest and to his left stand botanists John and

William Bartram, father and son. Philanthropist Stephen Girard and one of the orphan boys who studied at the Philadelphia school that he founded make an isolated pair.

In the lower left Thaddeus Stevens with his outstretched arm makes a commanding profile.

In the center of "The Apotheosis" is William Penn in colorful attire befitting his stature as founder. Benjamin Franklin and Robert Morris, two noted statesmen, stand on either side. All stand on a rock engraved with an admonition from the Old Testament.

For this canvas in the House, Abbey garnered distinguished men from Pennsylvania's history. By grouping them among patriotic and legendary symbols–American eagles and an enthroned Goddess representing the Commonwealth–the artist merged historical realism with inspiring ideals. For Abbey, blending the allegorical and the realistic was paramount in a public governmental arena.

For this unique setting of the Keystone State, William B. Van Ingen painted 14 round opalescent stained glass windows representing areas of commercial and cultural prowess in Pennsylvania at the turn of the century. Women with emblems for such areas as Bridge Building, Chemistry, Electricity and Education gleam brilliantly in the sunlight. Since the windows were cleaned, releaded and reglazed in the nineties, their colors are intense.

For the Representatives who bear a mandate from 12 million Pennsylvanians, the House Chamber offers challenging and inspirational themes in an exquisite Renaissance setting. ◉

◉ *Following pages: Supremely ornate, the House of Representatives Chamber is enriched by Corinthian columns and guilded arabesques against the colors cream and blue. Abbey's murals add to its sumptuousness.* ◉ ***Right:*** *Edwin A. Abbey's enormous mural titled "The Apotheosis" depicts "a perfect example" of state-building–several dozen male leaders in exploration, science, education and industry assembled at the feet of an enthroned goddess representing the Commonwealth.*

■ **Left:** *The featured artist in the House Chamber, Edwin A. Abbey, painted "Penn's Treaty with the Indians" for the south wall.*

■ **Above:** *"The Reading of the Declaration of Independence," is a realistic portrayal of this momentous event in America's story. On* July 6, 1776, Colonel John Nixon read the decisive document outside the Pennsylvania Statehouse. Abbey thoroughly researched his historical themes and had but one detail to complete when he died in 1911.

⊗ **Above:** Abbey's "The Camp of the American Army at Valley Forge" graces the north wall, showing the power of the imported Prussian leader von Steuben as he drilled poorly clad patriots in snowy weather. This created a poignant and popular image of the Revolutionary War. Bare wall panels surround this painting, which was originally planned for the Senate Chamber.

⊗ **Top Right:** In 1906, Architect Huston designed the Speaker's Chair, ornate with gold leaf, carved mahogany wood and hand-tooled leather. ⊗ **Right:** A scaffolding must be erected every two years to replace the light bulbs in the House chandeliers manufactured by Henry-Bonnard Bronze Company of New York. Each of the larger ones is said to weigh four tons.

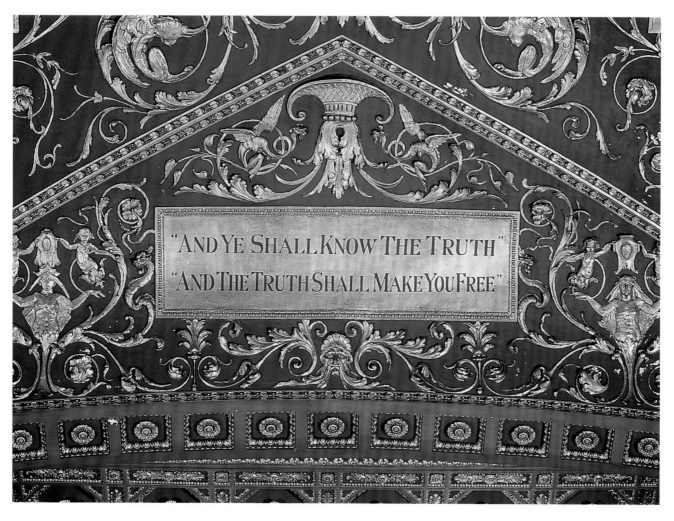

◼ **Top left:** "Religion" is one of the 14 stained glass windows in the House Chamber. Left: An inscription of admonition from the Bible is on a gilt tablet on the front wall of the House Chamber. ◼ **Above:** A continuous pendentive with ornate moldings meets the barrel vault with foliated bronze covering deep blue walls. William B. Van Ingen's round stained glass windows add deep brilliance to already richly decorated surfaces.

◉ **Previous pages:** *Elaborate classical details on the beams, columns and coffered spaces distinguish the House chamber. Architect Joseph Huston designed the sumptuous decorations of the 18 karat gilt candelabra.* ◉ **Top:** *In "Printing Press," a Van Ingen stained glass window, a young boy pulls a proof sheet.* ◉ **Above:** *Classical symbols-anthemion, palmette and entwined rope-decorate the entablature above the composite columns in the House Chamber. Bead and reel and egg and dart moldings are common in this American Renaissance structure.*
◉ **Right:** *In Abbey's oil painting in the center of the House Chamber ceiling, maidens representing each of the 24 "Hours" encircle a sky studded with heavenly bodies. The allegorical theme reminds viewers of the passage of the day.*

READING SOURCES

▣ Caffin, Charles H. **Handbook of the New Capitol of Pennsylvania.** Harrisburg: Mount Pleasant Press, 1906. This original guidebook by an English-born art critic reveals sources of the Capitol's design features.

▣ Heritage Studies, Inc. **The Pennsylvania Capitol: A Documentary History.** Harrisburg: The Pennsylvania Capitol Preservation Committee, 1987. A four-volume history of Pennsylvania's early capitals up to and including the design, construction, artwork and furnishings of the current Capitol.

▣ Huston, Joseph M., Papers of , including two scrapbooks of newspaper clippings, plus a scrapbook kept by R. Willis Fair, a member of the Capitol Building Commission, all in the Pennsylvania State Archives.

▣ Likos, Patricia. **Violet Oakley, 1874-1961.** Philadelphia: Philadelphia Museum of Art, 1979. An exhibit program presenting Oakley's life and works.

▣ Mercer, Henry Chapman, **The Tiled Pavement in the Capitol of Pennsylvania.** orig. rev. & ed. by Ginger Duemler. State College: PA Guild of Craftsmen, 1975. A captioned sketch of each pictorial mosaic taps into Mercer's knowledge of Native American and pre-industrial artifacts.

▣ Pennypacker, Samuel W. **The Desecration and Profanation of The Capitol of Pennsylvania.** Philadelphia: William J. Campbell, 1911. A Pennsylvania governor's view of the Capitol and its art.

▣ **The State Capitol of Pennsylvania** Harrisburg: The Telegraph Printing Co., 1926. A guide to the Capitol's architectural features and furnishings.

ACKNOWLEDGMENTS

I am deeply indebted to the staff of the Capitol Preservation Committee for sharing information that they have painstakingly garnered over the past years. My deepest gratitude extends to the Committee's Director Ruthann Hubbert-Kemper for her articulate knowledge and engaging enthusiasm for restoring a Capitol with a complex history.

Thanks also to Art Historian Keri Casey for identifying relevant material; to Historic Preservation Intern Carrie Forry for her cheerful gathering of documentation and to Secretary Elana Maynard for her kind coordination.

The Committee's restoration efforts benefit from the time and expertise of countless contributors. Among these, Architect Huston's daughter, Judelle Hunting, and her children as well as the owners of Huston's home "Oaks Cloister," Rev. Wilbur and Loice Gouker, have been invaluable sources of original correspondence, scrapbooks, artifacts and oral histories. Such contributions to Pennsylvania helped me understand the unfolding story of Huston's "Palace of Art."

I also thank my editor, Millie Rinehart, for her generous spirit and unflinching attentiveness to detail.

–Ruth Hoover Seitz